Beyond The Veil

Beyond The Veil

HOW TO GET TO THE PRESENCE OF GOD

Robert A. Parnell Jr.

One

INTRODUCTION

Ask anyone whether to experience more of God's blessings, like better finances, better health, or even just a happier life, and they will all quickly respond with a yes. I do not believe that a single person on this planet does not want to be blessed. We all want good things to come our way. You will be hard-pressed to find someone who will say, "I sure am wishing to get sick!" or "I hope my family is torn apart and I go bankrupt!" If we find someone who will gladly say those things, we quickly deem them purely crazy and foolish. Everybody wants blessings, but how many people are willing to do what it takes to get those tremendous and incredible blessings?

We tend to go to God with our list of wants. We approach His throne and begin to tell God all the things we want. We say to Him, "God, I want this and that, too." We go to Him with our hands open and almost act like God is somehow required to give us what we want. We want Him to provide us with everything but don't ever think about what is required of us. Jesus declares in Luke 10:2, "...*The harvest truly is great, but the labourers are few: pray ye, therefore, the Lord of the harvest, that he would send forth labourers into His harvest.* (KJV)" The house is full of people feasting at the table, but no one wants to do anything.

My heart desires to experience the blessings of God and live in the Shekinah glory presence of the Lord. Moses experienced the Shekinah glory as God instructed him to hide behind the cleft of the rock as God passed by. The residue or remnant of the Almighty God passing by caused Moses' face to glow. Stop for just a minute and think about that sentence you just read. Moses just saw what was left after God passed by, and it caused him to glow. What a mighty God we have!

But getting to that place in God will require something of us. That place where the pure or Shekinah glory dwells is reserved for those who have consciously decided to do and sacrifice whatever is needed to get there. You do not just happen to get to the Shekinah glory of God; instead, it is a determined effort that brings people of every race and status to this place. If you want more of God, then more of you is required to get to it.

This book is a 15-year journey in the making. I was preaching a mighty revival that had already gone for four weeks. The annual camp meeting was scheduled for the church's denomination that I was ministering in. The pastor decided to stop the revival for that week and asked me to start the revival again afterward. I agreed and even attended the camp meeting. During one of the evening services, the minister made a statement that completely caught me. He said, "It's time for us to go beyond the veil and experience God's presence." Immediately, I was carried spiritually to the Wilderness Tabernacle that God instructed Moses and the children of Israel to build. For the rest of the service, I heard nothing else. I was utterly captivated by God as He began to show me how to get into His pure Shekinah presence.

With each piece of the Tabernacle, God began to pour into me about what it meant in practical terms to experience His presence. From the gate to the Ark of the Covenant, I was carried and ministered to in a way that has forever changed my life. I went back to begin the revival again and began to minister upon what I had received. No one could have ever expected to see what I saw as people started to do what God had spoken to me about. I saw miracles and healing that defied human knowledge and medical science. Now let me finish that by saying this: TO GOD BE THE GLORY!!! I was simply the vessel that God used during that revival, but ultimately, God did the mighty works that were seen.

This book is not for the individual who has no desire to give and sacrifice anything else to God. This is intended for people who are tired of simply going through the ritual and motion. It is designed for people that desire to leave the normal or status quo and move into the extraordinary

and supernatural. It is for those hungry for more of God and desire to see what God will do. Jesus tells us in John 14:12, "*Verily, verily, I say unto you, He that believeth on me, the works that I do shall he also do; and* **greater** *works than these shall he do; because I go unto my Father. (KJV)*" We have not even scratched the surface of what God can, will, and desires to do in us and the world today.

I want to warn each of you that this journey we are taking together in this book will not be easy. You will be challenged and convicted in your spirit, just as I was, as you take this journey with me. You will laugh, shout, and cry during this journey. But suppose you will have an open heart and mind toward God and make a commitment and wholehearted decision that you will be different at the end of this journey than when you started. In that case, I can assure you will be surprised what God is getting ready to do for you and those that He uses you to touch.

As we begin this incredible journey toward God's Shekinah glory, I want to pray for you:

Heavenly Father, we come humbly into your presence. We come knowing that we are unworthy in and of ourselves to even come into your throne room. We come in the name of your son, Jesus Christ, who gave it all that we could have this privilege and honor. Lord, as we begin this journey to experience more of You, and Your power, let our hearts and minds be attentive and moldable unto you. Place us again on the potter's wheel and mold us into the image you created us to be. I pray for every reader, my team member, right now. Lord, let each of them receive of You so that they have never experienced You before. Let them receive power, strength, wisdom, and mighty anointing to accomplish the assignment of God in each of their lives. May the words of our mouths and the meditations of our hearts be acceptable in Your sight, O God, our strength, and our Redeemer. For we ask it all in Your Son, Jesus Christ's name. Amen.

I am excited that you have decided to come on this journey with me. We are partners and team members on this trip together. Are you ready to leave the normal and experience the supernatural? I am too. Let's go!!!

• Robbie Parnell

Note: All the scriptures used in this book will be from the King James Version (KJV).

Two

THE SANCTUARY

"And the LORD spake unto Moses, saying, Speak unto the children of Israel, that they bring me an offering: of every man that giveth it willingly with his heart ye shall take my offering. And this is the offering which ye shall take of them; gold, and silver, and brass, and blue, and purple, and scarlet, and fine linen, and goats' hair, and rams' skins dyed red, and badgers' skins, and shittim wood, oil for the light, spices for anointing oil, and for sweet incense, onyx stones, and stones to be set in the ephod, and in the breastplate. And let them make me a sanctuary; that I may dwell among them." Exodus 25:1-8

As we begin our journey together, we must start at the building of the tabernacle. Let's establish this fact initially: there is nothing that God does that is not on purpose and for a reason. The True and Living God is a God of details. This entire tabernacle that God instructed Moses to build was constructed with a purpose and motivation in the mind of God. Every part of the tabernacle led the people to the Holy of Holies, where the Ark of the Covenant and the Shekinah glory and presence of God dwelled.

I want you to notice that God instructs Moses to tell the people to bring the items and materials needed to construct and build the wilderness tabernacle. Could not God just provide the things by

Himself? Didn't He provide a ram in the thicket for Abraham when God told him to sacrifice Isaac? Why is God asking the children of Israel to bring the materials for the tabernacle?

Consider this situation for a moment. Which will a child take more care of and have more pride in: a vehicle given to them or one they had to work and save to buy? It will be the one they had to save to buy. They are invested in that vehicle. In His infinite wisdom, God understood that the children of Israel needed to give to be invested in this tabernacle. Though this would be the place that God dwelled, the children of Israel needed to be connected to this place as well.

If we are ever going to get to the presence of God, we have got to strive as well to be connected to God in a more significant measure. This comes from giving our time to reading the Word and praying, and talking to God. It even requires giving our finances to the work of God and being a worker for God in church and everywhere we find ourselves. As a pastor, I can tell you that many sit on church pews and are like little birds with their mouths open, waiting for someone to give them something. They are more than ready for God to pour out and give to them, but they haven't given God anything in years. They are the last person to volunteer and show up but the first to want something for free. The Apostle Paul declares to the church at Corinth in 2 Corinthians 9:6, *"But this I say, He which soweth sparingly shall also reap sparingly, and he which soweth bountifully shall reap also bountifully."* Simply put, what you put in is what you will get out.

Ask yourself, "What am I putting in for the Lord?" Now, be sure to be honest with yourself when answering that question. If the truth is told, for many of us, we try to fit God and His work into our schedule, and that just does not work. We will most certainly get too busy doing OUR agenda and simply push HIS work to the side. Many will justify it by saying, "The Lord knows that I have to get this done. He understands. I will do that for the Lord tomorrow." I will tell you honestly that I have been guilty of putting my work before God's work and have paid the price.

While in college, I experienced how putting God's work first makes a difference in one's life. A local church near my college had a pastor that had to work a second shift job during the week. This made it impossible for him to be able to attend Wednesday night services. He asked me to fill in on Wednesday nights. I was more than happy to help because I was a young minister. Sometimes it would occur that I would have a major test on Thursdays. Many of my college friends thought that I was foolish for going to church and preaching on those occasions. But I can attest to this: God always took care of me every time I put God's work first. I made at least 5 to 10 points higher than those that stayed and studied. You can never go wrong in giving to God.

Moses was told to take the offering from those that gave willingly. God is looking for people that will give willingly and gladly. The Bible tells us that God loves a cheerful giver (2 Corinthians 9:7). For too long, we have provided and done for God, many times, out of a sense of duty and out of the ritual and motion of it all. We do it because that is what we have always done. We do for God not because we willingly and gladly want to, but rather because it is the right thing to do. Grandma did it and told us we were supposed to, so here we go trying to make sure we don't make her upset. Challenging thought, but for many, it is their situation.

The fact is that we should willingly and gladly want to give everything we can to God. Why? Because He, when we as sinful man was lost and drowning in sin, sent His Son, Jesus Christ, to pay a debt that He did not owe because we owed a debt that was impossible for us to pay. A man that knew no sin became our sin for us. He was willing to endure such pain, shame, and agony for us to the rugged cross of Calvary. Just for that, we should be ready to give everything we have got to Him. How many times has He healed your body? How many times has He made a way where there was no way and answered prayer for you? Performed that desperately needed a miracle for you? The number of God's blessings to us is too numerous to know or tell.

We need to come back to the realization that we are the church. What we call "the church" is just the building or meeting place for the real "church." God's children are the church. We need to understand that God doesn't specifically need you, but we have the honor and privilege of being used by God. God could have chosen any group of people, but he chose the children of Israel. He, the God of the universe and every created thing desired to dwell among them. Let that statement sink in for you. He wanted to be near them. I wish to inform you that this has not changed. He still desires to be near you and me.

While we are no longer required to build a tabernacle like what Moses was instructed to build, there is a tabernacle that God requires of us, and it is ourselves. The Apostle Paul in 1 Corinthians 3:16 tells us clearly that we are the temple of God. There is a need to build our God a place inside of us, and that requires us to give the parts and elements to make Him a place to dwell in us. To have God's Shekinah presence, you must first give and build Him a tabernacle inside of you.

Every one of us has met or knows someone obsessed with making more money or climbing the corporate or social ladder. Oh, if they just once could see their name in the lights. The tabernacle that God was instructing Moses to build was the camp's focal point. The children of Israel would have a physical place to help keep their focus rightly centered. We, too, need to make sure that our desire and focus are rightly centered if we will make it to God's presence.

God has blessed me with a wonderful wife and helpmate and has given us two wonderful boys. Anybody that knows me will quickly tell you that I love my family and will defend them to the end, but my focus is higher than even theirs. My eyes are set on God, and my heart longs to be near to Him. I am not satisfied with where I am with God. I want more of Him, and God says, "If you want more of me, prepare me a place."

To prepare God, a place means that you have to dig a little deeper, give a little more, and work a little harder. God isn't looking for a place that is thrown together. He is looking for a place that has been carefully and deliberately constructed of the best that we have to offer. We all understand that our best does not even begin to compare to His best but thank the Lord that we are not held to that standard. God simply wants our best.

What are you giving Him? Is He getting your best or your scraps and leftovers? Are we giving God our full attention, or does He only have half an ear? Many years ago, there was a statement that became very popular. Everywhere was the word "WWJD: What Would Jesus Do." Though many took this as simply a fashion trend, some took this seriously to heart. Oh, that we would return to the place in our hearts and minds where God and having his presence would be the central focus of our lives. I desire to see the Children of God return to their love for God and his power and presence. Our world is in desperate need of the power of God. We need an old-fashion, Heaven sent, Sin chasing, devil stomping revival in America and around the world. The key to that revival is us.

We have spent enough time working on our wants and desires. More than enough time has gone to climbing the success ladder of this world and society. We have made sure that we are in good standing with the world and our community. Nothing is wrong with these things in and of themselves. We have taken so much time building up ourselves and very little time building for God in ourselves. Houses, cars, and anything you have physically will one day be gone, but that which has been obtained and built spiritually will forever stand.

Look around your spiritual house and tabernacle. Examine your walls. Look at the floors in each part and room. Even look at the ceiling of your spiritual tabernacle. What's on the walls? Are there pictures of yourself? Your accomplishments? Your position in the world? You see, we hang up on our walls what is most important and loved by us. Finding more of you and little of God on your spiritual walls is a clear and definite sign of your priorities and focus. We live in a self-centered world, and if we are not careful, we will fall into the world's pattern and not God's. It is easy to see that we live in a humanistic world that declares it is about us and not God. Count the pictures of Jesus. God, the miracles that He has done for and in you. Count the images of God's abundant blessings on you. Those pictures should vastly out-number the images of ourselves on our spiritual walls. We ALL have work to do concerning this.

How do the floors look? Are they kept swept? Are their things thrown all over them? It is hard to focus in the middle of a mess. The fact is that God and His mighty presence cannot effectively dwell in the middle of a mess. As we build the proper tabernacle for God in ourselves, we must consider every part of our lives.

I believe that it is time for some renovations in our tabernacles for God. Some areas of our lives need to be completely torn down and started again. The enemy of our souls has been chipping away at the very foundation of our lives for years. He has attacked our faith, peace, hope, and even our position with God. If we don't get this part right, the building of a place for God to dwell, the rest of this book is useless.

I want to make sure that what I invite God to dwell in is some-thing that I am not ashamed of. I want His place to be the very best that I have and can do for Him. I want Him to know that He is truly my central focus. I want Him to know that He is above all in my life. Can you say this for yourself as well? Is this your heart's desire too? Please know that rebuilding and fixing our spiritual tabernacles will not happen overnight. This will be a continual and gradual process undertaken with the knowledge that it will take God to help us.

The Psalmist pens it so well in Psalms 127:1 when he says, "*Except the Lord build the house, they labour in vain the build....*" God is the great architect, and he holds the master plans for the divine design of your tabernacle. If you and I will spend some extra time in the Word and prayer, He will reveal and show us the plans. I am not ashamed to tell you that I am still a work in progress. I am still building His tabernacle in myself every day, and the journey simply gets sweeter every day. Build Him a place to dwell, give your best to Him, and follow the divine blueprint, and you are walking your way to a closer relationship with God and into a position of His presence that is yet to be seen in your life.

Three

～

<u>THE GATE</u>

"And for the gate of the court shall be an hanging of twenty cubits of blue, and purple, and scarlet, and fine twined linen, wrought with needlework: and their pillars shall be four, and their sockets four. All the pillars round about the court shall be filleted with silver; their hooks shall be of silver, and their sockets of brass. The length of the court shall be an hundred cubits, and the breadth fifty every where, and the height five cubits of fine twined linen, and their sockets of brass." -Exodus 27:16-18

We are currently building God a place for His presence to dwell. Now, what's next? On this journey toward the presence of God, the element that we will encounter next is the gate. I want you to notice that the word "the" is used, and "gate" is singular, not plural. To this tabernacle, God instructed for one gate to be constructed. This gate would be 30 feet wide and 7.5 feet high. There would be one way in and only one way out. Please have an open heart and mind toward God as we continue our journey right here. This is where I had to pray, repent, and change how I lived my spiritual life at times.

To get to God's Shekinah glory presence, we must understand and acknowledge that there is only one way to God and His presence, and that is through Jesus Christ. Jesus declares in John 10:9, *"I am the door: by me, if any man enters in, he shall be saved, and shall go in and out, and find pasture.*" He also declares in John 14:6, "*...I am the way, the truth, and the life: no man cometh to the Father, but by me.*" I believe that scripture makes it clear that Jesus Christ is the only way and the true door to God.

This brings us to a problem that must be solved and fixed before moving further into the journey toward God's presence. What is that problem? The problem is that we must get over ourselves. Wow, that's a punch in the gut for many in the world today. Sadly, this is a problem in the church world today as well. We cling to titles, positions, and even years of service. Having evangelized and pastored for almost 30 years, I have been told by proud saints more times than I can count about how long they have served the Lord and all the positions that they have held. It is almost like trophies for them that they have proudly placed on their spiritual bookshelves. They are quick to tell you who they are and why you should know and respect them. Some naturally expect people to look up to them because of who they are.

Let's take a moment to examine who we are. We are fallen humanity that disobeyed and sinned against God. The Prophet Isaiah declares in Isaiah 64:6, "*We all are as an unclean thing, and all our righteousness is as filthy rags; and we all do fade as a leaf and our iniquities, like the wind, have taken us away.*" We are, of ourselves, unworthy and unlovable. We deserve punishment and Hell. Let us never forget that we were created from the dust of the earth.

Some of you may be saying, "Hey, that's getting a little too rough. You are messing with my self-esteem and self-image." I understand that place you are speaking from, but if your view of yourself is anything but humble and grateful for the undeserved blessings of God, then that bubble needs to be popped. What you and I have from God is not deserved or earned. We are simply the product of grace and mercy.

In a revival that I was preaching many years ago, a man told me all the good things he had done. He told me, "You see that parking lot out there. It cost $25,000 to have that done, and I gave $15,000 on it." He spoke with such pride and even told all the other "good" things he had done. He ended his long conversation with, "With all, I have done for God, there is no way He would send me to Hell." His problem was trying to get to God through the "gate of good things." As kindly as I could, I told him, "Sir, your good deeds will not get you in Heaven or buy your relationship with God. You must come to Jesus and repent and accept the gift of salvation through the shed blood of Christ. He is the only way to God and Heaven." This made the gentleman upset and aggravated, but the truth was spoken. It is Jesus Christ and the Cross of Calvary.

Some think this will be their door to God just because they hold positions. I have heard countless stories about ministers, spiritual teachers, deacons, and even evangelists and prophets who realized that their relationship with God is not established. One pastor talks about pastoring for 20 years and suddenly realizes that he was not saved. Wow, that is a sobering thought. Jesus declares in Matthew 7:22-23, *"Many will say to me in that day, Lord, Lord, have we not prophesied in thy name? and in thy name have cast out devils? and in thy name done many wonderful works? And then will I profess unto them, I never knew you: depart from me, ye that work iniquity."*

I have heard a phrase throughout my life that still rings true today. I have always been told that everything that glitters is not gold and everything that shimmers is not silver. Many that sit high right now will one day be brought low. They are trying to hold to a position to get them to God. They are trying to use the "gate of position and status" to gain access to God and His presence, but it will not bring them success. When viewed through the lens of God, people quickly see themselves as what they are: needy human beings that cannot hope to survive without God.

When people begin to understand and accept those worldly accomplishments, they do not gain you, or I access to God; it is the point that we start to turn in the right direction to get to God's powerful presence. I firmly believe that God is tired of His children walking around and living so pridefully. Let us be clear that I am not saying that we cannot be happy and rejoice in God over all that He has done for us, but we have no right to boast in ourselves over nothing. The writer of Hebrews instructs us to look unto Jesus.

I want you to understand that I am not telling you that you must live in a defeated mindset. I am not suggesting that you should not rejoice in all that God has blessed you with. I am telling you to let your focus and attention be on Jesus, the true Door. Our troubled world needs Jesus today more than ever.

In our journey toward God, we should be seeking to add people to this journey with us. When I was first getting into the ministry, I had an older minister that was a dear friend to me tell me that if I could get people to Jesus and the Cross, Jesus was more than capable of handling them from there. This might sound strange to talk about leading someone to Jesus to get the presence of God, but I will assure you that this is a vital part of this journey.

It goes back to giving to God from the last chapter. The more we work for God and witness to people, leading them to the True Door, the further we travel toward God. This gate was 30 feet wide, which is large enough to allow many in at one time. Are you leading people to Jesus, or are you satisfied with yourselves having the way? Here is what I have found out: the more I pour out, the more He pours in.

As the children of God, we should be shouting from the rooftops and everywhere we are that Jesus is the way to joy, peace, power, strength, and life. We should boldly tell the world around us about the gate that leads to God's presence. We should be testifying to our lost world.

Ponder on this: when is the last time you bragged on God more than yourself? When is the last time you paid more attention to God than yourself? Think of that for a moment and examine yourself and be honest with yourself when answering those questions. We all are guilty of spending more time on ourselves than on God; let's face the facts. We are more inclined to focus on ourselves than on Jesus Christ. In my ministry, I have witnessed God having done many miraculous things, and people will turn around and try to take credit for something that God clearly did himself. I am not condemning anyone for trying to take credit for things because it is our human nature to do things as such. But I am making it clear that the focus is on Jesus Christ because he is the door to God and the Almighty's presence.

We read in Matthew 14 a powerful story about the importance of keeping our focus on Jesus Christ. Jesus had spent a great deal of time ministering to a crowd of people. He had sent the crowd away and placed his disciples on a boat, instructing them that he would meet them on the other side. During this time, Jesus drew away to be alone and to pray. The Bible tells us that as the disciples were on the water, they saw this shadow coming across the water, and they heard the voice of Jesus when he said they take courage or be of good faith that it was Him. Peter would be the one that would say, "Lord, if it is you, bid me come to you." Jesus would tell him to come, and Peter would do the unthinkable and impossible to human knowledge: he would walk on water. Peter was fine as long as he kept his eyes on Jesus, but when he got his eyes on the waves and the wind that blew around him, the Bible tells us that he would begin to sink. It would only be when he put his eyes back on the master that he would start to walk again on the water with Jesus.

This story clearly illustrates and confirms that where we focus is essential. What we keep our eyes on makes a difference and tells where we are going. When you get in your vehicle to drive, you drive looking through the windshield. Nobody ultimately drives looking through the rearview mirror. If someone does try to drive all the time through the rearview mirror, they're going in the wrong direction. They're heading backward, not forward. It is sad to report that many in the church today are not forward moving, but instead, they are on a backward trend. That is sad to have to say, but all you have to do is take a moment and look around, and you can see it for yourself. Rather than people growing closer to God, they become more distant from God. And it is simply because they have decided to try to get to God through another means other than the True Gate, Jesus Christ.

A very popular group or event shows up at an arena or Coliseum near us, and tickets will sell out in almost hours. Drive by the nearest church on a Sunday morning, and there are still plenty of parking spaces to park in, and you can go to the church and choose where you want to see it because pews remain unfilled. It begs the question, what are we focusing on? That is a question that each individual will have to answer for themselves, but it is abundantly clear that we have forgotten about the Gate.

Life is full of distractions and obstacles that hinder many travelers on the road to God's Shekinah glory. The enemy of your soul will try to keep you interested in anything that will keep you from focusing on the true way. That is his job and let it not be mistaken that he takes his job very seriously. And if we're not careful, we will allow life to cause us to stop focusing on the Door and Gate. That is why you see so many walking around like they have been drinking lemon juice for the past ten years and preserved in vinegar. They have no joy, they have no peace, and they have no hope of anything better. They are the ones that complain all the time, and nothing that will ever be done satisfies them. You see, Jesus Christ is the only thing that will satisfy a hungry soul. Jesus Christ is the only way we will ever find the presence of God.

While we are preparing God a place to dwell, we need to make sure that the focus and the attention of that Tabernacle are placed on the right person. We need to ensure that we lead people to the source of all hope and blessings. We need to make sure that the cross of Calvary and the lamb that hung there are the central focus of our lives and our time and attention. Let me assure you that when we go through the gate by way of Jesus Christ, only blessings come our way, and the door to continue this journey toward the presence of God is opened wide.

Four

THE BRAZEN ALTAR

"And thou shalt make an altar of shittim wood, five cubits long, and five cubits broad; the altar shall be foursquare: and the height thereof shall be three cubits. 2And thou shalt make the horns of it upon the four corners thereof: his horns shall be of the same: and thou shalt overlay it with brass. 3And thou shalt make his pans to receive his ashes, and his shovels, and his basons, and his fleshhooks, and his firepans: all the vessels thereof thou shalt make of brass. 4And thou shalt make for it a grate of network of brass; and upon the net shalt thou make four brasen rings in the four corners thereof. 5And thou shalt put it under the compass of the altar beneath, that the net may be even to the midst of the altar. 6And thou shalt make staves for the altar, staves of shittim wood, and overlay them with brass. 7And the staves shall be put into the rings, and the staves shall be upon the two sides of the altar, to bear it. 8Hollow with boards shalt thou make it: as it was shewed thee in the mount, so shall they make it." -Exodus 27:1-8

After preparing for God a place to dwell and ensuring that our focus is upon the true Gate and Door, which is Jesus Christ, the next fixture before us is the brazen altar. This altar, which was seven and a half feet long and wide and four and a half feet tall, would be where the children of Israel would bring their sacrifice to God, and the priest would assist in sacrificing for the people. This sacrifice would be burned entirely. It would be done for the forgiveness and atonement of the sins of the children of Israel.

Again I will ask you to please have an open heart and mind toward God as we begin to deal with the practical application of this altar in our journey toward the Shekinah glory of God. With every step and part of this journey, the need to do self-examination and correction is even more vital. The further we go in our journey toward the presence of God, the greater the need is to be willing to continue to be molded by the hand of God and allow God to change those parts and areas of our lives that need to be changed. I can honestly say today that I am still a work in progress. I am far from perfect, and God is still working on me every day. Please do not think that I am even trying to suggest that I have arrived and have fully grasped and been wholly changed into what he has for me yet. At the beginning of this book, I said that we were team members on this journey. We are traveling together.

When we look toward the brazen altar and begin to examine its practical application to our lives today, we see clearly that a sacrifice was needed then and is still needed today. Now, some will say to me that Jesus Christ was the ultimate sacrifice. I do not argue that point; instead, I agree with that statement. At the beginning of the book, I said that if we were going to get to the presence of God, it was going to require something of us. Here, standing in front of the brazen altar is where something is significantly required of us: ourselves.

The Apostle Paul tells the believers in Rome in Romans 12:1, "*I beseech you therefore, brethren, by the mercies of God, that ye present your bodies a living sacrifice, holy, acceptable unto God, which is your reasonable service.*" In simple standard terms, the apostle Paul tells the Roman believers, "give God yourselves." The need for a lamb or a dove is no longer required, but the laying of ourselves on the altar is still a requirement. The question remains, how much of you have you laid on the altar?

This is also a rough and challenging spot for so many as well. We have dreams and desires, and we are indeed full of opinions. Have you ever met somebody that always knew everything how about everything and you could not tell them anything? I have met quite a few of them in my life, and unfortunately, they are some that sit on church pews every Sunday, and that description fits them perfectly. We must face the fact that we are a creation with strong opinions about many things. One of the biggest things that I have seen that married couples go through at the beginning of their marriage is that the husband and the wife have an opinion of how they think things should be done. And when the two cannot agree, there becomes a spot for a great argument. To be perfectly transparent with you, this was a sore spot for my sweet and loving wife and me at the beginning of our marriage. I had a way that I had done things for many years, and my wife had a way that she had done something for many years. We had to figure out how to compromise for our marriage and, not to mention, our sanity.

When it comes to dealing with God and our relationship with Him, there is no compromising when it comes to God's requirements and standards. As I have already stated before, God is a God of details. When God instructed Noah to build the ark, he gave Noah specific instructions to build the ship. When God gave Moses the instructions to build this wilderness Tabernacle, they were clear. They were so detailed that he told precisely how long, how wide, and where to place everything. So when we begin to come on this journey to get to the presence of God, we cannot cut a deal with God and compromise and expect to receive what God has.

The brazen altar for us, spiritually, requires us to put everything we are on the altar. We must come to a place where what we think becomes second to what God knows about it. We must place our opinions on the altar and put our time, efforts, and jobs on the altar.

We must be willing to lay aside what we want to do that which God desires to be done.

Let us speak clear today: we are a creation that has opinions and loves to be in control. If you will, many love to be control freaks. It is very well possible that you know some people that love to be in control of the situations that they are in. Some might say that they are just born leaders. Some might also say that they are just bossy by nature. But when it comes to the brazen altar, you must accept and acknowledge that you are not in control, and He is given all control of our lives. Many have no problem changing how they give to God, and many have no issues changing their focus toward God through the gate of Jesus Christ, but when we start talking about surrendering our will and our way, this becomes a deal-breaker.

We are attached to our thoughts both physically and emotionally. Surrendering our will is almost like trying to change our DNA. Have you ever had your mind made up for something, and someone tried to change your mind? How easy was it to change your mind? There are times when it is easier to change my mind than others. So I understand this struggle with surrendering everything to God.

I remember when I got my first $100 bill as a child. Everybody told me to save that $100 bill because it would be gone in no time once I ever used it. In my young mind, that simply sounded like foolishness. How could that much money be gone in the blink of an eye? To my surprise, when I used that $100 bill, in no time, it was gone. For me, that was depressing as a child. As I have grown, I have had times when I had money saved, and something would happen, and I had to use that money. I had plans for that money, and it was not what I had to spend it on, but I reluctantly handed the cash over and did what needed to be done. This is just like this spiritual journey that we're traveling. We have dreams and ambitions for things we want to do and see. And then we're standing in front of the brazen spiritual altar, and we hear God tell us that we have got to surrender at all and give it to Him. Those are hard words for us to hear as human beings.

This is a place where we need to ask ourselves whether what we have planned is better than what God, in infinite wisdom, has planned. We must understand that we are limited in our vision. We see things in two dimensions. We know the past and the present. God, on the other hand, sees things in three dimensions. He sees the past, present, and future. We are locked in the time of 24 hours, but God is dwelling in the time scheme of eternity. This simply means that God sees what you and I cannot see. We can only think about yesterday and live in today, but God can work in our tomorrow before we ever get there. Does it not make sense to give into the hands of that great God control of our lives?

I have gone into services of churches that I pastored and even preached revivals and had everything seemingly planned out. The service would start, and suddenly, my plans would have to change because God began to shift and work differently than I had anticipated. For some ministers, this is a hard place for them. For some, if you mess up their schedule, you throw them into a tailspin where they don't know what to do. God has done it to me so many times that I have become accustomed to changing my plans to accomplish his plans. To be honest with you, the best services that I have ever been in were the ones that my dreams were completely changed.

If you and I are going to get into the presence of God and dwell there, then we need to become accustomed to having our plans changed. That starts here at the brazen altar. You and I cannot be in control and expect to operate under God's power. That just does not happen. He is the leader, and we are simply His followers. Have we decided to allow God to have complete control of our lives? Have we laid everything on the altar of God and told He has complete control of it all?

Hear me very closely. I want you to understand that God is not looking for weekend visitation rights in our lives but rather for total and permanent custody. Many have given to God parts of their lives but have not entirely surrendered. Most people have a room in their house called the "junk room." It is the room where when you know somebody is coming that you throw everything that you don't have time to put up in its proper place. This is the room that you lock just to ensure that while somebody is going through the house, they don't mistakenly open that door. Likewise, in our spiritual house, we have a room many times that is locked, and we tell God he can walk into any room in our house except that room.

Check your spiritual house right now. Do you have a locked room in your house that nobody else goes into, even God? If you do, please understand that you are not the first to have it, and I can assure you that you will not be the last. It's time for us to unlock that door and allow God to come in. It's time for us to surrender that room to God and allow Him to use that space. When you submit everything to God, he receives all of your time, attention, and abilities. God is looking for wholehearted Christians and Saints. I believe that God is getting tired of people giving him only half of themselves. Only surrendering half to God simply means that you only receive half of the blessings that you could. You are cheating yourself out of blessings. I cannot speak for everyone, but I can speak for myself when I say that I want all that God has for all this for me.

The brazen spiritual altar still stands today. Unfortunately, many do not still go by it anymore. It is viewed as obsolete and a relic of the past for many. How wrong that they are!!! This sacred altar is still as needed today as it was in the time of Moses. There's a lot of boasting going on in our world, but not much humbling is being seen. Somebody is watching your life whether you know it or not. Somebody's watching how you walk and how you talk. My mother raised me with this thought: the only Bible that some people read is your life. What are they reading when they look at your life if that is the case? That is a sobering question and one that causes us to cringe at the moment. I have already told you that I am not perfect by no stretch of the imagination, so this question at moments can make me have to repent sometimes too. His time for us to lay it all on the altar of God, not holding anything back from him, but fully surrender ourselves to His Kingdom and service. It's time to get back to the brazen altar.

Five

THE BRASS LAVER

"And he made the laver of brass, and the foot of it of brass, of the looking-glasses of the women assembling, which assembled at the door of the tabernacle of the congregation." -Exodus 38:8

As we continue to travel on our journey to the presence of God, we now encounter the brass laver. Preparing a place for Him to dwell is complex and requires time. Laying ourselves on the brazen altar and surrendering everything to God requires commitment. But stepping up to the brass laver will be something that cuts and stings as we embrace its place in this journey.

This brass laver stands as a place of sanctification for the Child of God and traveler towards the presence of God. The term and idea of sanctification is something that is a mystery for some. It's something that they have never taken the time to think about. Webster's dictionary defines the word "sanctify" as "to set apart to a sacred purpose: consecrate, to free from sin: purify, and to make productive of holiness." In simplest terms, sanctification is the cleaning up of our spiritual temple and our lives.

Our God refuses to live in a dirty house. We cannot live for God on Sunday and for the devil Monday through Saturday. I know that those are hard words and maybe, for some, are very blunt, but we need to understand that a sanctified life is one that is lived at all times. We are all guilty of not living sanctified and holy lives all the time. We are all guilty of failing God in our lives. The writer of Hebrews tells us that without holiness, it is impossible to see God (Hebrews 12:14). It is sanctification that allows us to pursue after holiness and the presence of God. If we are ever going to get to the presence of God, it is going to require us to live holy lives.

Take a moment and think about your daily thought life. Do you know what is one of the significant reasons why preachers and ministers of the gospel leave the ministry? Do you know what is one of the most significant stumbling blocks for those that stand in the pulpit and declare the glorious gospel of Jesus Christ every week? It is our thought lives. The statistics show that ministers are some of the most addicted people to pornography. In my almost 22 years of pastoral ministry, I have tried out at churches where the pastor has had an affair with someone in the church and has left the ministry for them. Why am I telling that to you? It is for the fact that I want you to know that even those that sit in spiritual positions struggle with this brass laver and the sanctification that comes with it.

Now let us be very clear that if ministers and those in spiritual positions struggle, what makes us think those who sit in the pews will not battle with sanctification as well? Truth be told, we all are in need of a cleansing work of God. We all need God to cleanse us in areas of our lives. Not everyone struggles with the same thing, but let it be known that we all struggle with something.

Some people struggle with their mental lives. They're thinking about the wrong things. They have their minds set on worldly things. As a child, I loved to watch wrestling. Take a wrestling event from the 1980s and place it beside a wrestling event today. The females that you will see today are "almost" clothed. They are almost showing all their breasts, and the skirts that they are wearing leave very little to one's imagination. Why would that be? Because nudity or almost nudity sells. Let's face the facts; we live in a world full of lust. Turn on the television and watch any soap opera you want, and it will not take long for you to begin to see love triangles. There was a time in America that the most popular television show was the Andy Griffith show. We have long moved past that type of show. Television shows today are full of sexual ideas and promiscuous lifestyles. And there are many that sit on church pews on Sunday morning that is addicted to those type of shows.

We need God to clean up our minds. We cannot think about something for too long before it enters our hearts and becomes part of us. Let that statement sink into you. In essence, you are what you think. We cannot think about things that are against the standards of God's word and ever expect to be in the right relationship with God or ever to experience His pure presence in our lives. Many people live their lives with a mask on. They know how to act the right way, talk the right way, and act as a perfect model of a Christian. The outside looks terrific, but the inside is a total mess.

The Apostle Paul writes to the church at Philippi. He instructs them in Philippians 4:8, saying, "*Finally, brethren, whatsoever things are true, whatsoever things are honest, whatsoever things are just, whatsoever things are pure, whatsoever things are lovely, whatsoever things are of good report; if there be any virtue, and if there be any praise, think on these things.*" We must remember and understand that the mind is the enemy's battlefield. The enemy of our soul uses our mind to hinder and stop us on our journey toward God and His presence. If the enemy can make you think about something long enough, you will begin to believe it. Proverbs chapter 23 and verse 7 declares to us that whatever we think is what we are. Ask yourself a serious question of is what you think what you want to be. Or is what you are thinking leading you in the wrong direction.

Not only do our mental lives need to be cleaned up, but our

physical lives need washing and sanctifying. What we do in our day-to-day lives matters as well. Remember, I have already stated before that somebody is watching your life. As a minister, I have been into stores and places and did not figure that anyone there even knew who I was. But inevitably, somebody will come up and call me by name. No matter where I go, I have realized that there's always somebody there that knows me. We often do not think about things as simple as where we go and what we do, but this affects our relationship with God and can stop us very short of our goal of getting into God's presence.

Can somebody watch what you do and know who you serve? Are our actions progressing the Kingdom of God or hindering the work of God? We are either going forward, or we are going backward. We determine our direction. Our God is a God of free will. He is not standing there trying to shove anything down our throats. He gives us the ability to make choices, and with those choices come consequences. Galatians 6:7-8 tells us, *"Be not deceived; God is not mocked: for whatsoever a man soweth, that shall he also reap. For he that soweth to his flesh shall of the flesh reap corruption, but he that soweth to the Spirit shall of the Spirit reap life everlasting."* You cannot plant tomato seeds and expect to get watermelons. I know that that is a corny statement, but it makes the point very well. You cannot live unholy and unsanctified and expect to receive the blessings and opportunities of God reserved for those seeking holiness and true sanctification.

Every part of our lives must be placed in the light of God and His Word. The psalmist David asks God in Psalms 139 to search his heart and mind and if there was any wicked way to help him. Placing yourself up beside the standards of the word of God can be a scary thing. A sinful creation and lost humanity that has been redeemed by the blood of the Lamb, yet still striving and struggling at times, placing themselves up beside God's holiness is an unfair comparison. We can never fully attain God's purity and holiness in this life. It will only be achieved when we have reached our eternal home. But even if we can never attain to the fullness of the holiness of God on this side of eternity, we still must strive to reach that level of holiness.

I want to set the record straight on something that is misunderstood in the church world. Holiness is not a denomination; instead, it is God's standard for His church and the body of Christ. We often think of holiness as just a denomination, but if every child of God does not strive to walk in the life of holiness, they will end up away from God and away from the blessings of God. Let me also clarify that sanctification is not a one-time event, but it is a daily part of our lives. The apostle Paul talks about having to buffet the flesh daily. Jesus tells us that if we are going to follow him, we have to take up our cross and follow him. A phrase that I have heard all of my life is that Rome was not built in one day. Let me take that statement and apply that principle to you and me. Our habits and rituals of our lives did not happen overnight, and it will be a process to see them changed and made right on the side of God. Please understand that the things we are talking about in this book are not instantaneous; rather, they are things that we must work on daily.

I have often heard that in today's world, the church looks worldly, and the world looks more churchy. I do not fully believe that statement, but I will be the first to say that the church appears and acts more like the world than it should. There used to be a time when there was a clear distinction between the church and the world. There was a time when you could tell the difference between the two, but the line has become blurred in today's society. Have the standards and requirements of God for the church changed? Has God lessened what he wants from you and me? The answer to both of those questions is an absolute no. The writer of Hebrews tells us in Hebrews 13:8 that Jesus is the same yesterday, today, and forever. We have changed, but God remains the same.

Before the priest could enter the middle court that would lead to the Holy of Holies, he had to wash his hands and feet in the water of the brass laver. He had to make sure that his hands and feet were clean. Uncleanness was not allowed in the middle court of the wilderness Tabernacle or in the Holy of Holies where the ark of the covenant resided. For so many today, they have no problem coming into the presence of God any old way and expecting God to release His blessings on them. Please understand me. God wants the lost and his children to come to Him and bring their sins to be cleansed, but some have no desire to clean up and want God to take them as they are simply. We are once again back to where we want to be in control. We have already discussed that we are not in control, nor do we make the rules. God is the leader, and we are the followers.

I have had the privilege of being the pastor of many great Saints and soldiers in God's army. I watched what they did and what they said with watchful eyes and a heart open to God. I was fortunate that many of the seasoned ministers of the Gospel took me under their wing. They mentored me and have saved me many potholes on the road of the Christian life. Many of those seasoned ministers have since entered into their eternal reward. I thank God every day for every one of them that spoke into my life. One of the greatest lessons they taught me was that I must be on Monday what I was in the pulpit on Sunday. That lesson is one that you can apply to yourself even as a child of God. You must always be the same. Spending time at the brass laver will help you be consistently who God is making you into being. Spend some time washing in the Word of God. Allow the Spirit of God to help you in this journey. As you do this, you might be surprised at how you come out. Lord, change us and cleanse us so that we can be all that you have called us to be. How many will say amen to that? If we are to reach the presence of God, we will reach it through a clean and sanctified life.

Six

⌒

<u>THE HOLY ANOINTING OIL</u>

"Moreover the LORD spake unto Moses, saying, Take thou also unto thee principal spices, of pure myrrh five hundred shekels, and of sweet cinnamon half so much, even two hundred and fifty shekels, and of sweet calamus two hundred and fifty shekels, And of cassia five hundred shekels, after the shekel of the sanctuary, and of oil olive an hin: And thou shalt make it an oil of holy ointment, an ointment compound after the art of the apothecary: it shall be an holy anointing oil." -Exodus 30:22-25

After now walking through sanctification, which is a daily process of our lives and an essential part of this journey to the presence of God, we have made it to something that is also very misunderstood in the world today. We have made it to the holy anointing oil. You must understand that without the anointing of God in your life, you will never reach His pure presence. But let's talk about what the true anointing of God is.

Many have confused the anointing for someone's personality or charisma. We have all met people that were just tremendous speakers. These individuals can capture you and hold your attention till they get ready to let you go. I have had the opportunity to sit under some ministers who could captivate me, and I could sit there all day long and listen as long as they were talking and ministering. Is this something good to be able to have? I will say absolutely because nobody wants to listen to somebody boring. They lose our attention very quickly.

We need to understand that their ability to hold our attention cannot be called an anointing. If all a speaker has is personality and charisma, they are simply a great motivational speaker. The anointing is something that cannot be humanly replicated. The true anointing of God comes from God alone. The prophet Isaiah declares to us in Isaiah 10:27, *"And it shall come to pass in that day, that his burden shall be taken away from off thy shoulder, and his yoke from off thy neck, and the yoke shall be destroyed because of the anointing."* It is the anointing of God that will make the difference in the lives of His children. The anointing of God is what causes the blind to see, the deaf to hear, and the lame to walk again. It is that anointing that causes miracles to happen. We need that anointing working and moving in our lives. Let's examine the ingredients of this holy anointing oil that God has instructed to be made and see what we can learn from each part.

The first ingredient in the holy anointing oil is myrrh. Myrrh represents meekness. It comes from the trunk of the Commiphora tree in Arabia. It is produced in the form of tears. Alcohol will be added to remove any impurities. The gum will be steamed, melting it into oil, becoming a fragrance or perfume. Notice with me that this is produced in the form of tears. There is a myth that needs to be dispelled and completely broken. Men do cry. I know that comes as a shocker to many people, but real men do cry.

Let us be clear that humility or being humble is not a sign of weakness. If we want to be very honest, being humble and meek is a sign of being strong. The writer of Proverbs declares in Proverbs 22:4, *"By humility and the fear of the LORD are riches, and honour, and life."*

Even the Apostle Peter proclaimed in 1 Peter 5:6, *"Humble yourselves therefore under the mighty hand of God, that he may exalt you in due time."* Scripture is unequivocal in that God blesses and rewards those that live a meek and humble life. Our God does not respond to proud and boastful. As the children of God, we have never been instructed through the Word or in any other way from God to live high-minded. If somebody has told you that God said to be high-minded, they have lied to you. Would we understand that what we have is not because of you and me but because of God's grace and mercy. I have already stated before that what we deserve is hell, but what he gives to us is salvation through Jesus Christ by the way of the cross of Calvary so that we become citizens of a place called Heaven. But you won't get there proud, boastful, and high-minded.

The second ingredient in the holy anointing oil is cinnamon. Cinnamon represents uprightness before God and man. Cinnamon comes from a tree that grows approximately 30 to 40 feet high. The tree grows almost completely straight up without any noticeable curves. The tree leaves are taken and pressed, and the oil is used for cinnamon oil.

In the spiritual sense, to be upright is to stand and live the truth of righteousness and God's word. as I have already stated before, somebody is watching your life. What you do, where you go, and what you say does matter. We are either bringing glory and praise to God or bringing shame to His name. Please understand that I know that those are difficult words, yet they stand as reality. The way we walk through this journey of life matters.

Some have a way of walking and living right in front of people, but their lives are entirely different in secret. Their secret life will be brought out and into the light somewhere along the way. I challenge you to examine your life right now as you are reading. Be truthful and honest with yourself when looking at every part of your life. Is every area of your life upright before God? Are you standing for truth in every area of your life? If we are to reach the presence of God, then we must achieve it by walking uprightly before God.

The third ingredient of the holy anointing oil is calamus. This ingredient represents humility. Calamus is a reed that is grown in the swamps. The oil is found in the head of this reed. You know that it is ready to be harvested when the reed is bent over almost in half—a perfect symbol of humility.

Humility is hard to find in today's world. The majority of people are proud and bold in proclaiming who they are and what they've done. You often hear statements like "a self-made millionaire" or "a self-made man or woman." it is built into our sinful human nature to want to take credit for things. We want to be accepted by society and the world. We do everything in our power not to be part of the outcast. We act as if we did it all ourselves and maybe have even convinced ourselves of such. The truth remains that we haven't done anything that is successful outside of the hand of God.

I believe that proud saints that walk around like a peacock with its feathers unfurled is something that runs people away from the church rather than to the church. I am not telling you that you cannot be proud that Jesus Christ died for your sins and has saved you, but I am telling you that you and I have no right to think we're better than anyone else. We are all human and have come from a sinful past, but thanks be unto God, we have been redeemed and brought out into the light of almighty God. God is looking for humble children that will humbly come and willingly work for the Kingdom of God. You cannot reach the presence of God without being humble before God.

The fourth ingredient in the holy anointing oil is cassia. Cassia represents cleansing. It is produced from the leaf of the senna plant. It is still used today for inner cleansing—how we so desperately need cleansing in our world today.

Cleansing goes right along with sanctification. I have already said that sanctification is a daily process. Anybody who thinks that they are spotless and no more cleansing is fooling themselves and has been lied to by the enemy. There are areas of our lives that need to be cleaned up. None of us have yet to reach perfection, and until we are perfect, there will always be room for cleansing. My prayer daily is for the Lord to clean me up and help me walk a clean and sanctified life. However, I must admit that I do not always succeed in this desire. Just because I failed today, does it mean that I stop on this desire to the Lord. God is calling all of us back to the cleansing fountain whereby we can be washed daily in His presence.

The fifth and final ingredient in the holy anointing oil is olive oil. Olive oil represents the Holy Spirit. Are we allowing the Holy Spirit to have free will in our life? Are we allowing the Holy Spirit to shift and change those things in our lives that need fixing? We are people of habit, and we do not like change. Many become very upset when plans or things change. If we are going to be anointed of God and complete our journey to the presence of God, we are going to have to allow the Holy Spirit to lead us. Is the Holy Spirit leading you? It is a serious question to be answered.

This anointing oil that we have talked about in this chapter is vital to reaching God's pure Shekinah glory. To walk in this anointing will require something of the individual. It requires one to be willing to become an enemy on the enemy's hit list. You can count on being attacked, persecuted, and talked about. Walking under this anointing will place you under the eyes of skeptics, unbelievers, and even jealous Christians. Many want the blessings and power that come with this anointing, but unfortunately, they are unwilling to pay the price for it. This is the place where each of us must decide whether we are determined and committed to this journey to the presence of God. The ultimate question right now is, where do you stand? Are you willing to endure whatever it takes to receive this anointing from God? If so, prepare yourself, perform the parts of this anointing oil in your life, and prepare for the most incredible journey of a lifetime.

Seven

TABLE OF SHEWBREAD

"Thou shalt also make a table of shittim wood: two cubits shall be the length thereof, and a cubit the breadth thereof, and a cubit and a half the height thereof. And thou shalt overlay it with pure gold, and make thereto a crown of gold round about. And thou shalt make unto it a border of an hand breadth round about, and thou shalt make a golden crown to the border thereof round about. And thou shalt make for it four rings of gold, and put the rings in the four corners that are on the four feet thereof. Over against the border shall the rings be for places of the staves to bear the table. And thou shalt make the staves of shittim wood, and overlay them with gold, that the table may be borne with them. And thou shalt make the dishes thereof, and spoons thereof, and covers thereof, and bowls thereof, to cover withal: of pure gold shalt thou make them. And thou shalt set upon the table shewbread before me alway."

Exodus 25:23-30

We have prepared ourselves through the outer court of the wilderness Tabernacle. The journey has been challenging and convicting along the way. Because of our preparation, we have now entered the middle court. You must understand that many people are satisfied hanging around the outer court. They talk of journeying into the middle court one day, but that day never comes. So count yourself as one of the faithful minority or remnant that you have reached the middle court. You can see the veil that brings you into the Holy of Holies from this place. People talk about the veil, but they never see the veil. You can call these kinds of people the boat sitters. We find ourselves in a position of walking by faith.

Here in the middle court, you will find three more steps to get to the ark of the covenant and the presence of God. We start here in the middle court with the table of shewbread. This table represents the Word of God. For years, the Bible has been the number one bestseller on every bookselling list. Though it has been a best-seller, there was a moment when another book took its place for a while. The book that would take the Bible's place would be the Harry Potter series. Whether or not you like this book series, for it to take the Bible's place as the best seller is disturbing. To think that Wizards, magic, and sorcery would become more interesting than learning about the true and living God. For me, it simply shows where we are today. For so many, God has become a second thought.

I saw a video a few years ago that the pastor had done in New York City. This video was to be used to introduce his message on a particular Sunday morning. With a camera and microphone in hand, this pastor set out to walk the streets of New York City and ask simple Bible questions. When I asked who built the ark, most people said Moses. The question was asked what Sodom and Gomorrah were. To this question, people would answer that they were a married couple in the Bible. The pastor would ask where Jesus Christ was born, to which most could not even answer. The purpose of the video was to show how biblically illiterate our world is today.

Most people can quote the very first verse of the Bible and even know John 3: 16 by heart. They can quote for you, "Jesus wept." Yet beyond this, they know very little. People will sit for hours reading romance novels, books about history and periods in the world, and any other subject you want to even think about, but they have no interest when it comes to reading God's word. How can you live a Christian life and not know what God's word says?

When football players are practicing for a game, they must learn the different plays for the game. Baseball players must learn hand signals from their coach to know whether to run, steal a base, or stay. Every sport has plays, and players must learn those plays. God's Word gives Christians the plays and directions for a successful life with God. Without knowing the directions, how can we complete God's course and destiny for each of us?

If we are to reach the presence of God, we must fall in love with the Word of God again. We must learn again how to feast upon it. Inside its pages is soft food to sustain us and tough food that must be chewed on. This is where we have a problem. The Word of God will change you, convict you, and expose you to yourself. Our human nature does not like change, and we surely do not like to be told we are doing wrong and have it shown to us in front of our eyes. That's why so many people take the Bible like a buffet. As with a buffet, where people can decide what they put on their plate by what they like or do not like, we want to hand-select what we want to read and accept by what is convenient and feels good to us.

Let me make this as clear as I can for all of us right now. The Bible is not a buffet, and we do not have the privilege to validate parts of the Bible as accurate and other parts as not valid. You cannot cherry-pick what you want from the Book. From Genesis to Revelation is the God-inspired, God-breathed, inerrant and holy Word of God. You and I will not stand before God and be judged by man's law nor man's books. When we stand at the Judgement bar of Christ, we will be judged by the Word of God. So, it behooves us to make sure that our lives align with what God has said.

How much time do you spend searching the scriptures and learning about God? I understand that we have so many things that take our attention and time in our modern world. It comes down to desire and priorities. I will be the first to admit to you that sometimes my priorities get out of line, and then God has to come along and convict me through His Holy Spirit for me to fix my priorities.

I want to show you how people's priorities get out of line. We can sit down and watch a two-hour movie, but it is almost agony for some to sit in church for two hours. Going to the store and spending $20 is seemingly nothing, but it seems like a fortune to some when putting it in the offering plate. We can even change our plans on a moment's notice, but if a church event has to be rescheduled, you better give at least three weeks' notice. And we wonder why we do not have power? God is seemingly the last thing on our minds.

Inside the pages of God's Holy Word, I find hope, strength, peace, and answers to life's problems. When we are weak, God sends His word to give us strength in those moments. When we find ourselves in places spiritually that we do not understand, it's through the Bible that God will provide us with divine directions. I must say that I have found the Word of God to be the best GPS in the world. It needs no updates, and it's always perfectly accurate. Following God's Word will place us exactly where God desires us to be.

The workload at our job gets heavy, and our home life becomes more and more stressful. We get into a mode and ritual of life. We have a routine and schedule that we follow in our day-to-day lives. It's early to rise in the mornings and late to bed at night trying to finish up the loose things of our day. We become so busy that God and time with Him are not even considered. It doesn't mean that we are bad people. It doesn't even mean that we are sinners. It only means that we are individuals that have got our priorities out of line. When I take the time to get in His Word in the mornings, my day goes so much better. Many people I know have a routine of reading right before bed. They say it helps them gain strength and peace as they go to sleep. The idea is it doesn't matter if it's in the morning, in the middle of the day, or as you're going to bed. The only thing that matters is spending the time feasting upon His Word.

One of my church members from one of my former churches introduced me to what he described to be the meaning of the word Bible. He told me that the word Bible meant the basic instructions before leaving earth. It is an old saying, but it has stuck with me. I find instructions in the Word that tells me how I should live and what I should do in every circumstance of my life. The bookshelves of the bookstores are jam-packed and full of self-help books. They tell you they are five steps to this and ten steps to that, and they're flying off the shelves daily. People are eager to devour and read every word of those books, but they forget about the book on the bookshelf in their home collecting dust.

It is time for us to dust off that Bible that sits on the coffee table or the shelf in the corner and begins to reread it. The world we live in today would indeed be a better place if we spent more time reading God's book and less time reading man's book. Imagine what would happen if we spent more time in the Holy Word. Hospitals most certainly would be more empty, families would be more peaceful and together, and the enemy of our soul would be even more scared of the body of Christ than he is today. We need the Word of God more today than ever before. A challenge for each of you to dare. I challenge you to give God the time by searching the scriptures and see for yourself if your life isn't sweeter and more harmonious than ever before. Take the time to read the Book.

Eight

THE GOLDEN LAMPSTAND

And thou shalt make a candlestick of pure gold: of beaten work shall the candlestick be made: his shaft, and his branches, his bowls, his knops, and his flowers, shall be of the same. And six branches shall come out of the sides of it; three branches of the candlestick out of the one side, and three branches of the candlestick out of the other side: Three bowls made like unto almonds, with a knop and a flower in one branch; and three bowls made like almonds in the other branch, with a knop and a flower: so in the six branches that come out of the candlestick. And in the candlesticks shall be four bowls made like unto almonds, with their knops and their flowers. And there shall be a knop under two branches of the same, and a knop under two branches of the same, and a knop under two branches of the same, according to the six branches that proceed out of the candlestick. Their knops and their branches shall be of the same: all it shall be one beaten work of pure gold. And thou shalt make the seven lamps thereof: and they shall light the lamps thereof, that they may give light over against it.
Exodus 25:31-37

Another item found here in the middle court is the golden lampstand. As we look toward the lampstand, we see a representation of the light of God. One candle was not enough. God called for seven candles, which signifies perfection. On this journey toward the presence of God, we must look inside of ourselves and determine if the light of God is shining as bright out of us as God desires. Let's take a moment to decide honestly how bright God is shining out of us.

Are we a 25-Watt bulb? Does there appear to be a dim light shining but not enough to light the way before us? I submit to all of us that many today are dim in shining the light of God. They have become too bogged down in life's mess that the troubles and situations they face block God's light in their lives. It is a matter of their time and attention that causes the light of God to be dim. These are the individuals that find themselves on a significant spiritual roller coaster. These are the people who it can be up on the highest spiritual mountain at this moment and be on rock bottom in the next 10 minutes. Their light is not bright enough to keep them lifted.

Maybe we find ourselves as a 50-Watt bulb. The light is shining just a little stronger, and the path in front of us is slightly easier to see but still very cloudy. This person has learned how to deal with their situations of life partly. Their roller coaster does not have quite as many highs and lows, but they still struggle just to survive. We find these individuals that have their feelings on their shoulders. It doesn't take much to offend them. Honestly, throughout my over 21 years of pastoral ministry, I have encountered quite a few of these people. I have told people before that I did not know when I accepted the call of ministry that I also needed to be a certified firefighter. These 50-Watt bulb people are the ones that get offended and mad, and the pastor has to go to put out the fires that have started because of their offense. They are good people, but they are very fragile people. They allow things and other people to hinder the light of God in their life.

Some might find themselves as a 75-Watt bulb. The light is a lot easier to see, and the path is getting brighter that maybe others can follow in our journey as well. They are more stable and confident people. They find that their roller coaster is more straight than up and down. These individuals will have highs and lows as any other normal human being will, but they are more stable than the others we have talked about. These will be those that can be described as wishy-washy at times. They have a strong love for God and a desire to serve the Lord, but the newest trend or thought can easily persuade them. They are in church for three Sundays and out for two. Though they love the Lord, they still allow situations and circumstances to hinder them. They will help for the next fundraiser but may not be there for the worship service next Sunday. As a pastor, I can honestly tell you that the church world is full of these kinds of people. Somewhere along the line, we have lost the spirit of commitment. I thank the Lord that there are still some in the church that can still be counted on to be there every time needed. My prayer is that these 75-Watt bulb people will become more committed people.

Then there are the ones that find themselves as 100-Watt bulbs. Their light is shining brightly for the entire world to see. These individuals are the ones whose light is so bright that anyone who comes in contact with them can easily follow the path they are walking. These individuals are the ones that you can count on being there every time it is needed. If you will, I call these the fateful remnant of the church. These are the workers, prayer warriors, Sunday school teachers, and worship leaders. These are the ones you can count on in any circumstance that you need them. Let us be clear that these individuals still have the highs and lows like anyone else in life, but with the light of God that shines so brightly out of their life, they can, with God's help, navigate through all the situations that face you and me in life.

I have briefly summarized the four types of bulbs that shine out of you and me. I did not go into a deep conversation concerning any of them, but I went through enough that if you look at yourself, you can see where you fall. If you fall below the 100 Watt bulb, please do not be discouraged. I would say that all of us fall into the dimmer light at different times. I can honestly say that my light for God does not always shine as brightly as it could or should. We are all guilty of not shining the light of God as effectively as we are called to do.

With that being said, we must look inside of ourselves and figure out what is dimming our light. We must begin to self-examine ourselves and be honest with ourselves and what is causing us to not be as bright for God as we should be with His light. It could be a job, and for others, it could be marital or family issues. The number of causes is more than can be named here and covers various situations. It is up to us, with the help of God, to figure out what is our situation and hindrance and allow God to help us fix and remove every obstacle.

The world we live in today desperately needs to see the light of God shining out of every one of us. The world today is a dark place full of chaos and confusion. It is a place where it truly is a "dog eat dog" world. Our younger generation is killing themselves one after another, and drug and alcohol abuse is rising daily. Sadly, most of the church world is sitting back and watching everything happen and not even trying to do anything to stop it. I am thankful for the remnant that is standing up and trying to do something for the Lord in the midst of our world. We need more children of God to stand up and make a difference, but how can you stand up if your light for God is shining bright enough for people to see?

If we are ever going to make it to the presence of God, it is going to require us to work on the light shining out of our lives. We will have to work on the light of God in us. You must understand that your children, grandchildren, nieces and nephews, and family and friends desperately need to see the light. It is time we quit waiting on someone else to do it, and we step up and do it. It is time that we quit thinking that it is only the job of the preacher or minister to shine a bright light and begin to understand that every child of God must shine brightly for the Lord.

This light must shine not only on Sunday but also on Monday

as well. This light that I am talking about is not just something that you wear on special occasions, but it is something that you must have every single day of your life. Situations can dim the light in our lives, actions, and words. Many do not understand that the light is affected by everything you do in your life. The closer you are to God, the brighter you will shine, and the farther you are from God, the less you will shine. Unfortunately, many today are down to just a tiny flicker of light. If we want the presence of God, then we need to do some serious work in our lives to make sure that is light is shining as brightly as it can. Jesus said in Matthew 5:16, "*Let your light so shine before men, that they may see your good works, and glorify your Father which is in heaven.*" As disciples of Christ, we are called to let the light shine. God has given us the ability to shine, so I tell you that it is time to begin to become brighter for God and dimmer for the world and its attractions. The presence of God in your life depends on which you choose.

Nine

GOLDEN ALTAR AND INCENSE

*And thou shalt make an altar to burn incense upon: of shittim wood
shalt thou make it. A cubit shall be the length thereof, and a cubit the
breadth thereof; foursquare shall it be: and two cubits shall be the
height thereof: the horns thereof shall be of the same. And thou shalt
overlay it with pure gold, the top thereof, and the sides thereof round
about, and the horns thereof; and thou shalt make unto it a crown of
gold round about. And two golden rings shalt thou make to it under the
crown of it, by the two corners thereof, upon the two sides of it shalt thou
make it; and they shall be for places for the staves to bear it withal. And
thou shalt make the staves of shittim wood, and overlay them with gold.
And thou shalt put it before the vail that is by the ark of the testimony,
before the mercy seat that is over the testimony, where I will meet with
thee. And Aaron shall burn thereon sweet incense every morning: when
he dresseth the lamps, he shall burn incense upon it."*
Exodus 30:1-7

*"And the Lord said unto Moses, Take unto thee sweet spices, stacte,
and onycha, and galbanum; these sweet spices with pure frankincense:
of each shall there be a like weight: And thou shalt make it a perfume,
a confection after the art of the apothecary, tempered together, pure and
holy: And thou shalt beat some of it very small, and put of it before the*

testimony in the tabernacle of the congregation, where I will meet with thee: it shall be unto you most holy. And as for the perfume which thou shalt make, ye shall not make to yourselves according to the composition thereof: it shall be unto thee holy for the Lord."

Exodus 30:34-37

On our journey to the presence of God, we have finally come to the last object that we must face to get to the presence of God. We have come to the golden altar that sits directly in front of the veil to the ark of the covenant. I find here at the golden altar that there are two representations of requirements to get to the presence of God. These steps are essential, but this step is necessary and vital to you and me getting to God's pure presence.

The first representation that I see here is that the golden altar also represents Jesus Christ, our intercessor. At this altar, incense is burned, going up to God as a sweet smell. We have sitting at the Father's right hand, someone who is constantly putting up to God our request and needs in the same way that this incense goes up to God. This brings us back to one of our starting points on this journey. We have already identified that the gate to this wilderness Tabernacle signifies that Jesus Christ is the only way to God. Here we find again that Jesus Christ is mentioned again. We must understand that we will never reach God or His pure presence without His son, Jesus Christ.

To just imagine that constantly in the presence of the throne room of God is constant intercession going on for you and me. While we sleep, our elder brother continually talks to the Father for us. No matter what the need is in our lives, there is always somebody praying for us. When you and I slip and fall and make mistakes, as we most certainly will, an intercessor is constantly talking to the Father for us. Your forgiveness came by way of this intercessor, and your healing will come by way of this intercessor. Doesn't that make you want to rejoice? Does that make you want to say "Hallelujah"? When you do not have another friend you think is with you, we can be confident that Jesus Christ is always there.

By all of the things that Jesus Christ does for us as our intercessor, it brings me to the other representation of this golden altar. At this altar, as already stated, incense is going up before God as a sweet-smelling savor continually. This incense that is going up represents our praise. And if we do not have something to praise Him for, something is wrong inside ourselves. There should never be a time that you and I should not have something to praise him for. I have preached throughout my ministry that if all you have is your salvation, then eternity is not long enough to praise him for simply that.

Somewhere along the line of our lives, we have lost the spirit of praise. The spirit of praise has been replaced with the spirit of griping and complaining. We are more like the children of Israel in the wilderness than maybe we even realize. We have no problem finding everything wrong with everything in our lives. Seeing the negative side does not take much time. When it comes to finding the positive or the bright side of the situations in our lives, we struggle at times just to find one good point. We wonder why people do not want to come to church. The answer to that question is a straightforward one. The answer is that they can look around the world and get the complaining, but what they need from us is to see some praising.

There is power in your praise. There is strength in your praise. There is joy in your praise. There is peace in your praise. The list could continue to go on and on of the great things that come through our praise. Praise takes effort from us. Praise takes commitment when life is going sideways. Do we have the determination and commitment to praise Him even when we don't feel like it, or the circumstance does not humanly call for it?

In Second Chronicles chapter 20, we find that nations were rising against Israel. You would think that Israel would send their best fighting warriors into the battle. The best fighting warriors would only make common sense to you and me to be the first into action, but that is not what God would speak through the prophet to King Jehoshaphat. God would instruct the king first to send the praise team or worship singers into battle. Scripture will record that as praise began to go up to God, the warriors of the other nations began to fight each other. Israel will never have to fight or lift their sword one time. God will fight the battle himself simply through their praise.

I believe that people forget how powerful praise is. I have had many times in my life that I have had to praise my way through circumstances and situations simply. When you begin to praise, God begins to listen. Psalms 22 declares to us that God inhabits the praises of his people. So when I start to praise, God bends down from the throne and begins to listen to me intently. When you begin to praise God, the enemy of your soul begins to run the other way. God and the enemy can't dwell together for too long.

Look across the church world today and, even more specifically, look across your local church and watch how many come in as if they are the most hopeless people in the world. They drag in, and they drag out. There is no smile, and there is no joy in their lives. Many times the problem is they have lost their praise. Somewhere they forgot that when praises go up, the blessings of God come down. They have forgotten that praise can change our circumstances and situations. Just ask Paul and Silas in the Roman jail. At the midnight hour, which is the darkest moment of the entire night, they began to sing praises unto God. The Bible declares that the ground would shake, and the chains that hailed them and the other prisoners came off at all the prison doors were opened. Locked up in your praise could be a blessing and miracle for someone else.

We must understand that the world needs to see our praise. The lost and dying among us need to see the children of God lifting the highest praise to the God of the heavens and the earth. They need to see that there is still praise on our lips even amid the most significant trials of our lives. When the pain of situations and circumstances surround us, and we barely feel like we can breathe, the world still needs to see praise being lifted from the children of God. If we are to reach the presence of God, then we must begin to praise Him with everything that we have within us.

The old praise chorus says that I will enter His gates with Thanksgiving in my heart and enter his courts with praise. Praise is not optional; instead, it is required of the child of God. This proves to be a problem for many people today in our world. With so much negativity around us, it is easy to become negative as well. We must guard ourselves against becoming a negative people. Negativity is contagious and can be caught by others if we are not careful. Today, many churches go through the ritual and the motion because they have forgotten how to praise.

The way that you and I are to praise is as simple as opening up your mouth and simply telling God thank you. Praise is something that is not hard to continue if you start. When you start praising him for waking you up, it's not difficult to praise him for the other many things that he has done for you and is accomplishing for you. All it takes is someone willing to lift praise. If we want to get to the pure presence of God, then let the Saints of God lift up praise again to God.

Ten

❦

THE HOLY OF HOLIEST/THE ARK OF THE COVE-
NANT

"And they shall make an ark of shittim wood: two cubits and a half shall be the length thereof, and a cubit and a half the breadth thereof, and a cubit and a half the height thereof. And thou shalt overlay it with pure gold, within and without shalt thou overlay it, and shalt make upon it a crown of gold round about. And thou shalt cast four rings of gold for it, and put them in the four corners thereof; and two rings shall be in the one side of it, and two rings in the other side of it. And thou shalt make staves of shittim wood, and overlay them with gold. And thou shalt put the staves into the rings by the sides of the ark, that the ark may be borne with them. The staves shall be in the rings of the ark: they shall not be taken from it. And thou shalt put into the ark the testimony which I shall give thee. And thou shalt make a mercy seat of pure gold: two cubits and a half shall be the length thereof, and a cubit and a half the breadth thereof. And thou shalt make two cherubims of gold, of beaten work shalt thou make them, in the two ends of the mercy seat. And make one cherub on the one end, and the other cherub on the other end: even of the mercy seat shall ye make the cherubims on the two ends thereof. And the cherubims shall stretch forth their wings on high, covering the mercy seat with their wings, and their

faces shall look one to another; toward the mercy seat shall the faces of the cherubims be. And thou shalt put the mercy seat above upon the ark; and in the ark thou shalt put the testimony that I shall give thee. And there I will meet with thee, and I will commune with thee from above the mercy seat, from between the two cherubims which are upon the ark of the testimony, of all things which I will give thee in commandment unto the children of Israel."
Exodus 25:10-22

The journey has been long and at moments, there has been quite a bit of soul searching and conviction as we have made our way toward the presence of God. Now we are going beyond the veil into the very place where the presence of God dwells. We are stepping into the Holy of Holies. I want you to understand that many never reach this place in their spiritual journey. Many are satisfied living outside in the outer court or the middle court. It is the dedicated few that will do what is required to reach the pure presence of God. I have preached throughout my ministry that the presence of God and His anointing comes at a price.

You need to know that coming to this place will make you disliked but many in the church world today. Dwelling in this place will put you on the enemies hit "list." You need to understand this because some reached this place and become surprised when the enemy started to attack them even more. But thanks be unto God that when you dwell in this place with God, you are armed with more power than any enemy or devil can withstand. Dwelling here is the ultimate desire of our God for His children.

This presence of God that we find here is the power to see people healed, delivered, and set free. We find in this place that the power is given to the children of God to see miracles beyond our imagination. Again I want to repeat that those who do not commit to getting to this place will be jealous of you. Prepare to be talked about, ridiculed, lied about, and shunned. I want you to understand the gravity of being in this place entirely. Because many do not have the desire and commitment to make it here, they're going to resent you for committing to making it to this place with God.

As you understand that thought and reality, I want to tell you that what God will do with you far exceeds anything they can even imagine or think about. I want you to come to a place where those that talk about you become just chatter and noise in the background. There is a great work that must be done for our God in these last days and hours that we are living in. I don't have time to get bogged down in what people think or say about me; instead, I must be busy with "my father's business."

God is looking for people and servants that He can freely use. It is beyond the veil that we become the most effective for the Kingdom of God. It is beyond this veil where the power can rest upon us to see the divine purpose of God entirely and wholly fulfilled in our lives. You must understand that many do not understand this power that I speak of. Human nature causes us to doubt what we do not understand. So people will quickly dismiss this power because they simply do not understand it. I don't have to understand it; I just need to have it operating in my life.

This power that is found beyond the veil is vital as you work on your job, as you go shopping, and simply walk down the street. When you walk in this power, God will begin to send even more people in your direction that need a mighty touch of Him in their lives. You become a living and breathing instrument in the hands of the almighty God. There is no devil, situation, or circumstance that this power cannot see you through and see lives changed to the glory of God. He will find that those in need will be seemingly drawn to you like a magnet. For some people, this becomes surprising and alarming. They don't understand Hal people just suddenly become attracted to them. What a wonderful thing it is that our God would trust and honor us with this power to be used to see people's lives changed.

This power will also change your life. You will no longer see things the same way you've always seen them. You will no longer desire the things that you used to want. Your life's mission and goal will radically change as you begin to let this power from beyond the veil saturates your life and have His way in you. I know that if one person in a church finds themselves beyond the veil and is enabled with this power, it can change an entire church. Salvations begin to happen. Holy sanctification begins to become a desire, and the Holy Ghost becomes the most welcomed church member. What is flowing in you can change everything around you.

Let's face the fact that the world is looking for real change. Our world is looking for a genuine experience, and sadly they are not finding that inside the doors of our churches. Our churches have been relegated down to a form and a fashion or a ritual and motion. The saved show up at the church, and the sinners stay home in their beds. Please understand that I'm just trying to be honest with you. What we have now in the majority of our churches will never bring forth what God has for the body of Christ. We desperately need this power from beyond the veil to see the will of God accomplished not only in our lives but in our world today.

I desire to see a remnant of people who become "power getters." These are committed to getting all God has for them and releasing it into our world. Nobody ever said that it would be easy, but I can promise you that it will be worth it all to see our lost loved ones and those around us saved and changed and full of the power of God. I have the mindset that if nobody else wants to go, that's not going to stop me from going. This power from beyond the veil will call the spiritually dead to come back to life again. I pray that you have the same desire that I do, and that is to receive of our God everything that he has for us.

As a child, I remember how the power of God flowed in the churches all around me. I remember the Saints of God praying with everything they had in them for the lost and undone and watching as those they prayed for came home to Christ one by one. The Saints of old had tapped into the power that is beyond the veil. Today's problem is simply that we have prioritized our time toward ourselves and not toward God. But if you have walked with me all this way, that is a clear sign that you desire to do and see what the Saints of old saw and even more incredible.

Plain and simple, it's time to quit playing church, and it's time to have church. It's time to stop talking about God and begin experiencing God again. It's time to stop talking about what God has done in the past and begin to worship and celebrate what he's doing right now in our lives. It takes a while to make it to the veil, but it is worth every step to get here. We have an obligation to our children, grandchildren, and all those coming behind us to make sure that this power that is found beyond the veil is not lost or forgotten.

That has been my purpose for writing this book that you now hold in your hand. I purposed in my heart to write this book so that anybody who would read it could understand to be able to apply it practically to their lives. I pray that I have succeeded in my mission to do so. I am hungry for more of God and our desire to draw even closer to him than ever before. Many searches for success in what this world can afford them, but my heart cries out for success with God. Our God is thrilled when one of his dear children finds their way beyond the veil. I pray that that space beyond the veil would begin to fill up more and more.

I began us with a prayer, and I want to leave us likewise:

"Heavenly Father, we come to you this day, and we thank you for the blessing of Your power and presence. Father, this journey has not been the easiest, and at times it has been difficult as we have had to search for ourselves and admit that we have fallen short of where we should have

been. Today, we recommit ourselves to following after You and allowing You to have Your way in our lives. Forgive us for our sins, and forgive us for all the undone places in our lives. Help us become closer to You than ever before, and allow us the privilege and honor of being used to see Your glory spread worldwide. Help us do our part and fulfill the mission and call You have placed on all of our lives. Lord, we will thank you and praise you for it all. In Jesus' name, we pray. Amen.

May the grace of God go with each of you, and may you never stop seeking the power of God in your life. Remember, somebody's watching your life, and what you do, somebody will copy. May they copy a God-filled powerful life.

In Christ Jesus, I Stand Complete,

Rev. Robbie Parnell